Regards from the DRAGON

George Lee

Compiled By David Tadman

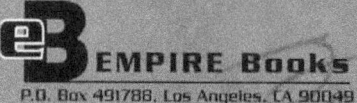

EMPIRE Books
P.O. Box 491788, Los Angeles, CA 90049

To George,

You are the greatest!

Bruce Lee

Regards from the DRAGON

George Lee
Compiled by David Tadman

EMPIRE Books
P.O. Box 491788, Los Angeles, CA 90049

Disclaimer
Please note that the author and publisher of this book are NOT RESPONSIBLE in any manner whatsoever for any injury that may result from practicing the techniques and/or following the instructions given within. Since the physical activities described herein may be too strenuous in nature for some readers to engage in safely, it is essential that a physician be consulted prior to training.

Copyright © 2008 by WALK ON LLC.
Published in 2008 by Empire Books

All rights reserved. No part of this publication may be reproduced or utilized in any form or by any means, electronic or mechanical, including photocopying, recording, or by any information storage and retrieval system, without prior written permission from Empire Books.

Empire Books
P.O. Box 491788
Los Angeles, CA 90049

First Edition
08 07 06 05 04 03 02 01 00 99 1 3 5 7 9 10 8 6 4 2
Printed in the United States of America.

Library of Congress Cataloging-in-Publication Data

ISBN-13: 978-1-933901-44-2
ISBN-10: 1-933901-44-6

Lee, Bruce, 1940-1973.
  Regards from the dragon / [collected] by George Lee ; compiled by David Tadman.
    p. cm.
  ISBN 978-1-933901-44-2 (pbk. : alk. paper)
  1. Lee, Bruce, 1940-1973--Correspondence. 2. Lee, George, 1917---Correspondence. 3. Martial artists--United States--Correspondence. 4. Teacher-student relationships--United States. I. Lee, George, 1917- II. Tadman, David, 1965- III. Title.
  GV1113.L44A35 2008
  796.8092'2--dc22
                       2008020650

Cover photo courtesy of David Tadman.
Cover & Interior Design - Mario M. Rodriguez, MMRDesign Solutions

LEGAL NOTICE
The name, likeness, image, designs, symbols, and trademarks of, or associated with, Bruce Lee are owned by and used with express permission of Linda Lee Cadwell and Concord Moon LP. All rights reserved.

Dedication

I would like to dedicate this book to the memory of Bruce Lee, my teacher and friend, and to the spirit of jeet kune do.

To be sure, Bruce was a true innovator of life. One does not have to study martial arts to experience the art of Bruce Lee's philosophy. Jeet kune do can be found in the songwriter's songs or the painter's paintings.

Bruce Lee did not believe in styles or doctrines, nor did he believe in set patterns. He believed in self-examination and self-realization, both of which lead to truthfully expressing one's self. The name jeet kune do is only a group of words to remind you that you are in the process of self-exploration.

So, to all the martial artists and painters and songwriters, I also dedicate this book to you.

George Lee

Editor's Note

With the exception of a few private comments from Bruce Lee, these letters were transcribed just as he wrote them.

George Lee: "The Master Maker"

George Lee was more than a good friend of the legendary Bruce Lee; he was a revolutionist in his own right. He spent countless hours that turned into days and sometimes months, creating Bruce's workout equipment.

For George's hard work, dedication and expertise, Bruce called him "The master maker." In addition to this accolade, George should also be known as the "The Master of friendship," because his reliability, dependability and friendship were unparalleled.

Thus, to George Lee, a dedicated friend and a man who always truthfully expresses himself, this book is also for you my friend.

David Tadman

Acknowledgements

"To share with family and friends is to be fulfilled."

There are several people I would like to thank, starting with my wife, Mary. She has shown me incredible support and love through all the years we have been together.

I would like to thank Linda and Shannon Lee for their inspiration and friendship. My appreciation can't be measured in words. They conquered many obstacles with love, compassion and understanding; they are true heroes.

I would like to thank David Tadman for inspiring me to do this book. David composed this book out of love and the search to know more about a man he calls his hero, Bruce Lee.

I would like to thank the following people for their love and support in doing this book and the desire to know more about their hero Bruce Lee. Steve Walling, Tsuyoshi Abe, Steve Kerridge, and John Kreng.

Finally, I would like to thank all the wonderful family and friends I have had the privilege to share precious times with.

George Lee

Contents

FOREWORD BY GEORGE LEE ix

REFLECTIONS OF BRUCE xii

REGARDS FROM BRUCE LEE 1

LETTERS OF APPRECIATION 63

GEORGE LEE 69

CAPTURED MOMENTS 77

A SPECIAL DEDICATION 109

IN CLOSING 111

Foreword
By George Lee

I met Bruce Lee in the early 1960s and from the time of our first meeting up until his passing in 1973 we remained good friends.

To me, Bruce Lee was a very special person on many fronts. He was a revolutionary in the world of Martial Arts as well as a philosophical prophet. He was a man with a vision, and he let nothing stand in his way of accomplishing that vision. Bruce Lee was a self-made man, and he made his dreams reality.

I was very fortunate to have known Bruce. I was truly blessed to have shared precious moments with him and to be included in his search of himself his art and his life.

Bruce Lee can never be compared to any other martial artist or philosopher. He was truly in a league all his own. What made him great was the journey he took in self-discovery and self-determination. Bruce saw his goals and willed those goals, And in the end, he always accomplished what he set out to do.

Bruce was determined to let nothing stand in his way. In fact, I believe he welcomed obstacles to be in his way. He knew that if he overcame these problems, it would make him stronger and more determined in his path of self-enlightenment.

Bruce's Teaching Philosophy

Years before I met Bruce, I studied Kung-Fu. When Bruce came into my life and opened my eyes to his way of training, I knew then that all my previous martial arts training was obsolete. I put all my past training aside and became a disciple, so to speak.

I was some years older than Bruce. Therefore, at first, it was strange that this young man was teaching me. However, it only took a few lessons for me to realize that this he was doing something special. Bruce was able to relate to people - regardless of age, race, religion - in a way I have never seen. when you took his class, all those things did not mean anything. And you, as an individual, were the same as everyone else.

Bruce and I had many lunches and dinners together, and we conversed about a variety of topics, including martial arts to philosophy. Bruce was a truthful and giving man that truly wanted the best for you.

He not only taught you the physical and philosophical side of the martial arts, but also the psychological aspects. He always wanted you to be prepared in every situation. On several occasions, I remember walking into class and - without any warning – he screamed my name. Without giving it a second thought, I would respond with a loud yell, "Yes!" That was simply Bruce's way of keeping you on your toes. He would always do little things like that to keep your awareness up.

It seems now, in retrospect, that Bruce had seemed to conquer the mental, physical, and-almost-the spiritual. I say almost because he was in the process of doing so when unfortunately he passed away. I believe that if one conquers these three levels in life then one will conquer himself.

Bruce's Training Equipment

My friendship with Bruce went beyond the training we shared. We also collaborated in the construction of the many pieces of equipment he used for his personal training. Bruce would come to me with an idea for training equipment, and I would make his vision come to life.

I am truly honored that I was an important friend in Bruce's life and that I had contributed in his expression of his physical being. Bruce and I spent countless times designing equipment and going over diagrams and ideas that gave that equipment life. When they were completed, he used them in his daily training.

When I see Bruce in his films, I feel proud that his physical stature had something to do with the equipment that I made for him. Bruce was truly serious about his physical training. The equipment I made for him helped him in his search for a better, stronger and healthier body. Bruce put his trust in me and felt he could share with me one of the most important things in his life: the development of his physical being. I feel honored that he put that trust in me, and I truly miss those times we spent together, creating the machines that helped him in his search for physical perfection.

The Unforgettable words

When Bruce was becoming more famous in the world of television and film, we saw less of one another. Despite his hectic schedule, however, he always kept in contact with me via letters.

Throughout the years that Bruce and I shared as friends, he would occasionally send me letters that touched on a variety of topics, including his career, his martial arts and physical development, the machines I built, or equipment he wanted me to build for him. Most all, these letters show just how much Bruce appreciated me as a friend.

The letters in this book show much more than Bruce Lee the film legend, Bruce Lee the martial arts legend or the philosophical prophet. These unforgettable words show Bruce Lee the human being, the friend and the artist who was in search for self-expression. I held on to the memorable words in these letters for years, occasionally looking at them and remembering the special times they represented.

Nowadays, you can go to a bookstore and find many publications on Bruce Lee, from his martial art training to a memorial tribute. I believe all these books help keep Bruce Lee's legacy alive.

In this book, however, I wanted to show Bruce from a different perspective. Thus, When you read these letters, picture them as personal correspondence from Bruce Lee to you. By doing this, you will get a small glimpse into what I experienced as his student - and most of all - his friend. So read this book not as an outsider, but someone who shared in the experience.

George Lee

" To share ones riches is to enrich others"

Relfections of Bruce

Meeting Bruce

It was back in the early '60s, '62 or '63 I believe. How it happened was, I belonged to a dance club with Bob Lee who was the brother of James Lee. We heard that Bruce knew Hong Kong cha cha, so we sent for him from San Francisco to see what he knew. The Lee brothers got him to come out here to give a demonstration on Hong Kong cha cha, and that's how I met him. What impressed me most about Bruce at that time was, during intermission from the cha cha dancing; he put on a martial arts demonstration. I was incredibly impressed because I had never seen anyone as fast as he was. When the class demonstration was over, I approached Bruce and asked him what kind of martial art he was doing. Bruce told me that it was wing chun. I told Bruce that I have been training in gung –fu for the past 15 years and have never seen anything like he was doing. Bruce told me that he was going up to Seattle and when he got back he would be happy to teach me his style of martial arts. Bruce eventually came back and we rented an old broken down house in Oakland, where he started to train students. I believe we started with about four- to-six students for his class.

The Teacher and the Student

To be accepted as one of Bruce's students there was a process you would have to go through. He would screen everybody in the beginning and ask them questions like, why do you want to learn martial arts? If you would reply with anything violence oriented, Bruce would decline you as one of his students.

I remember a great story with Bruce and a couple of Oakland police officers. Bruce was really this skinny young guy and he had to weigh no more than 120-125 pounds at that time. Bruce lined up these two Oakland officers that had to be about 220 pounds each. Bruce did the one-inch punch on them, one at a time and he knocked each back about ten feet. That was pretty amazing. Bruce always impressed me as this fast-as-lightening, strong-as-an-ox type of guy.

When Bruce taught you, he taught you with simplicity and fluidity. He was also very strict at times. He would show you something once or twice and if you did not get it, he would be more aggressive with you. This type of thing was not meant for intimidation, but only for the fact that Bruce would really believe in you and wanted you to believe in yourself. He was great that way. Bruce was very easy to get along with and very down to earth guy.

I had trained in martial arts most of all my life. I trained in China in the art of gung-fu, but we called it Northern style or Southern style back then. When I started training with Bruce, it made all my other experiences in the martial arts obsolete. What Bruce taught me was very applicable to life and different situations that might come up. What I learned in China was just the opposite. He would always stress to me that what I have learned before him was strictly classical movements. It was like I woke up and found out what I had learned for over 15 years was in a way meaningless. I would have to say it was the fluidity and the simple ness in how he taught that attracted me. He was a great teacher.

One time, Bruce showed me some moves that were not taught to the majority of the students, and I was told to keep it to myself. Bruce did feel that there was not one person the same, so therefore each individual might need different teaching. When Bruce taught me, I was some many years older than him and it made me feel very young and what I had learned before really did not work for me anymore. What Bruce was teaching was so far out of this world and so different, I said to myself this is it, and this is the ultimate.

Bruce was able to break down the age barrier, what he did at that time was revolutionary. He opened the boarders for all races and religions. Many protested about this, but he wanted to teach the world. He was a true teacher and took many risks.

Listening to Bruce and learning from him at such a young age was almost surreal to me. It was amazing that he knew so much about the martial arts and life in general at such a young age. I remember when we got together, Bruce would break out the old boxing films and go over them with us. I really feel that this is where Bruce got his foundation – from boxers. He would always say to me, never fear a big man but never underestimate a small man. He would also tell me when you strike someone or something, it should be like a wave that rolls and hits its target with crashing force. I remember Bruce used to light a candle and snuff it out with the back of his hand from two-to-three feet away. Now that is a lot of force.

Enter the Equipment

I can remember the first time I made Bruce a piece of equipment. Bruce would take payments from the students and would really have no place to put the cash. It was kind of disorganized, so I made him this great-looking box with handles on it. It was made from stainless steel. Bruce was very impressed and was amazed at the job I did. From that time on, I made his equipment. Those are great memories. Bruce would draw out what he liked and I would make it. Bruce was a great sketcher and he could draw amazing pictures.

One time, Bruce sketched out a pair of nunchaku and when I made the pair, I added extra length to each of the sticks. I think Bruce and I were the originators of the now popular-sized nunchaku. I made many pairs for Bruce until he was completely satisfied with the weight and size. He was an incredible perfectionist. I remember making the first pair with some type of cord connecting them, and then I made a chain with rings and put then together. That was Bruce's favorite. Bruce was incredible with them. I got pretty good but never as good as he. I have to mention another piece of equipment that I made for Bruce, and that was the forearm-gripping machine. Bruce came to me and said he had to build up his forearms with strength and speed. I designed a gripping machine for him that would not only build him mass, but also stretched his forearm muscles at the same time. This is why when you see Bruce's forearms in different pictures; you can see all the definition in his arms. That machine was made for his complete forearms. He used to love that thing.

I made for Bruce countless workout equipment that he used on a daily basis like many different punching and kicking bags. First we filled the bags with rice, and it did not feel right to Bruce, so then we put BB pellets in the bags and they were too stiff. We eventually ended up with Mung beans.

Many of the equipment I made for Bruce was truly ahead of its time. What Bruce and I started was something raw and ground breaking. I am proud that I have created such machines, that over 20-to-40 years later all these big companies are doing their own versions. I guess we were innovators. I feel

very proud that I played a very important role in Bruce's life. It was an honor for me. When I see Bruce in his films and I look at his body development, I can see my equipment did its job. For example, I made machines that would target more than one muscle in Bruce's forearms. This is why you see so much definition on him. Others might have great forearms, but they might not be working out with equipment that targets all the muscles in that area. It really depends on your equipment and how you work that body part. Bruce had good equipment and he worked at it very hard.

There is one piece of equipment that I feel heartfelt about and sad at the same time. Bruce wanted me to make an ancient Chinese axe for a film he was to start after "Enter the Dragon", a type of Chinese period film, but with his improved martial art for film. Unfortunately he never had the chance to see it, because he passed away. He really wanted that Chinese axe badly.

The Oakland years

In Oakland we are all like a team and we were all very compatible with each other. We would all go to lunch together and celebrate each other's birthdays. We were definitely like one big happy family. There was never any animosity toward one another. At that time, myself, Allen Joe, Jimmy Lee and Bruce Lee were together all the time, it was like being the Four Musketeers.

Jimmy Lee was a tough guy; he was a real street fighter. He was so tough that you could punch him anywhere on his body and it would not hurt him. Bruce liked Jimmy a lot, because he was tough and Bruce had a lot of that in him as well. They got along great, and Jimmy, like the rest of us, were sort of big brothers to Bruce. When Jimmy passed away Bruce was devastated. Jimmy taught a lot of the classes when Bruce went to Hollywood to do his acting. Let me just say that Bruce and Jimmy's teachings were different in the sense that Jimmy was more aggressive and had a hands-on approach.

Bruce was always fun to be around. He would always joke around and be the life of the party. Bruce would always do a lot of different tricks, like drop a dime in your hand and then change it with a nickel before you could close your fist. He was so fast, he used to do that trick all the time. Bruce would always be moving, he would never sit still. He would be walking down the street and kick the leaves on a tall tree or he would punch signs. He was always moving and training. There was never a dull moment with him.

In Memoriam

I have countless fond memories of Bruce Lee, the lunches and the dinners and all the times we shared together as friends. To me, Bruce was a very special man. He would come up to visit me and I would go see him in Los Angeles. He taught me to break boards at his house there, in the backyard. Those are great memories for me.

Bruce Lee was one of a kind and he was a giant among the martial artists, he was simply the ultimate in my opinion. Bruce tried to stress the importance that Jeet Kune Do is not just for the martial artist, it is for the painter who paints or the musician who plays music, it is a way of life and for me it is simplicity of life and the centerline that Bruce Lee always taught us in class.

If I were to give any message to the Bruce Lee fans of the world, it would be to respect yourself and your limitations, and always truthfully express yourself. Always remember that Bruce's energy is with us all...

"Friendship is a gift, a gift that never stops giving, and when the friend is gone, it then becomes heaven sent..."

In Memory

In recent times, two of our brethren in the Jeet Kune Do world have passed away and have been mourned by many that were close to them, as well as the people they touched worldwide if it were just for a few moments. Both Herb Jackson and Larry Hartsell were an important part of the world of Bruce Lee for many reasons. Yes, I can talk about the enormous contributions Herb made with helping with some of the creations of equipment Bruce used, or I can talk about the incredible technician / fighter Larry was, but as the years go on, you, the readers of this book, will find out things about these men time to time about just how important they were to the world of Bruce Lee, and I supposed I will learn more as well about these men who I knew.

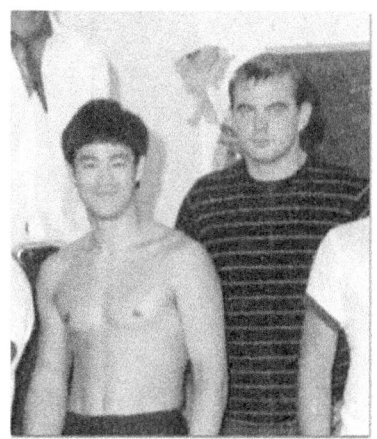

The most important thing is, is that we remember these men as contributors to what Bruce Lee was trying to achieve, they were an extension of his teachings and stayed loyal to Bruce up until their passing. They both were honest and humble and would do and go out of their way to help their fellow man.

I feel comfort in knowing that these two men are now training along side their Sifu in the heavens above.

God Bless both of them…

Regards from Bruce Lee

In the early 1060's, George Lee met an amazing man – Bruce Lee. George Lee and Bruce Lee became friends on many different levels. There was the teacher-student relationship, the artist-creator relationship and most of all, there was the close friendship they had until Bruce Lee's passing in 1973. On the following pages, you will experience the closeness these two men shared.

Letter 1

Description of Letter No. 1

In his letter, Bruce always used to tell me what was happening in his life. When I look at this letter, I remember great moments of going out to eat with him and discussing the martial arts, as well as how his career was going. Bruce and I shared many moments like this.

Transcription

Dear George,

I'll be going to New York on the 1st of May then to Wash. D. C. for an appearance. After that, I'll go to Seattle for two days and will stop by Oakland for a day before returning home. It will probably be on May 10 that I'll stop by Oakland. At that time let's get together and have a Gung Fu session.

The latest is that Greenway Production will most likely pick up my contract – a one year series is in the planning.

Take care,
Bruce

Left to right, Bruce Lee, Van Williams and Jhoon Rhee at the Jhoon Rhee Karate Championships 1967.

Dear George,

I'll be going to New York on the 1st of May then to Wash. D.C. for an appearance. After that I'll go to Seattle for two day and will stop by Oakland for a day before returning home. It will probably be on May 10 that I'll stop by Oakland at that time let's get together and have a Gung Fu session.

The latest is that Grunway Production will most likely pick up my contract —— a one hr. series is in the planning.

Take Care.

Bruce

Letter 2

Description of Letter No. 2

When I read this letter, it takes me back to the time when Bruce and I hung out together at Wally Jay's luau. Good friends and great conversations always surrounded times like that.

Transcription

Dear George,

I'm planning to come up for Wally's luau and at the same time to go to James' class in Freemont. Understand that class consists of mostly Chinese. I'll fly up on Friday (Nov.3) and James class is that same night. So if you have nothing previously Planned, it might be beneficial for you to attend that class. I'm going to teach a public class – it has been a long time. Say, maybe you can go to the Luau too.

Anyway, I'll talk to you when I'm up there. If you like to attend the Freemont Class for this night, contact James.

Take care my friend,

Best regard to your wife.

Bruce

Sifu Bruce Lee top center, George Lee picture left at James Lee's house with the Oakland branch gung fu class in Jimmy's garage early 1966.

Dear George,

I'm planning to come up for Wally's leave and at the same time to go to James's class in Fremont. Understand that class consist mostly Chinese.

I'll fly up on Friday (Nov 3) and James class is that same night. So if you have nothing previously planned, it might be beneficial for you to attend that class. I'm going to teach a public class ---- it has been a long time. Say, maybe you can go to the leave too.

Anyway, I'll talk to you when I'm up there. If you like to attend the Fremont Class for that night, contact James.

Take care my friend

Best regard to your wife

Bruce Lee

Letter 3

Description of Letter No. 3

Bruce was excited about the possibility of getting a role on the television show "Hawaii Five-0." Unfortunately, that never materialized.

Transcription

Dear George,

Your work, everyone of them, is fantastic. Not only are they professional, they are simply artistic. As usual, everyone here has high praise for your art. I myself, do appreciate very much for your taking time off to do all those wonderful things for me. Thanks a lot George.

I'm sorry to say that I've lost your list for Autograph. So will you please send me another one. Tell Dave Young of the delay too.

Upon my arrival, my agent called to let me know of CBS, proposal for a one hr. serial – kind of like I spy called "Hawaii 5-0." Looks good. Will let you Know what develops.

Will probably start tour next month but somehow or another will drop by one weekend for a Gung Fu Session.

Thanks again for everything and do not forget to send me the list.

Bruce

A promotional still shot of Bruce Lee promoting the Green Hornet, autographed and on occasion given out by Bruce Lee to his family, friends and fans.

Dear George,

Your work, everyone of them, is fantastic. Not only are they professional, they are simply artistic. As usual, everyone here has high praise for your art. I, myself, do appreciate very much for your taking time off to do all these wonderful things for me. Thanks a lot George.

I'm sorry to say that I've lost your list for autograph. So will you please send me another one. Tell Dave Young of the delay too.

Upon my arrival, my agent called to let me know of C.B.S. proposal for a one hr. serial — kind of like I Spy called "Hawaii 50". Looks good. Will let you know what develops. (over)

will probably start tour next month but somehow or another will drop by one week end for a Gung Fu session.

Thanks again for everything and do not forget to send me the list.

Bruce

Letter 4

Description of Letter No. 4

I always liked the letters I got from Bruce that discussed the equipment I had made for him. I am truly happy that I could be part of his life in such an important way.
We shared countless hours developing this equipment so he could improve his method of exercise, which set the path to his physical greatness.
I also made many signs for Bruce. They were like little affirmations he would hang on the wall or put on his desk. Those were great times.

Transcription

Dear George,

Masterful! Simply masterful! Dan and Linda are stunned when they see the Yin/Yang symbol. They said it's way better than the other "professional sign" given to me by Allen. Like I said previously it is very very artful.

Also, I must thank you for the name plates and the stainless steel card container – they are the Greatest! My deep appreciation for your time and thoughtfulness.

First of all, I like you to mail me your membership card at your earliest convenience.

The drawing on the bottom 1st. page gives the exact measurements. In comparison to a human head, the width 7" is from ear to ear, the height 3 3/8" is from forehead to top of the nose, and the deepness of 1" is from front of head to back of head. Now to the bottom part, the neck, as on a human. The height 3 1/8" is from under chin to bottom of neck above collar bone, the width 6 5/8" is from the end of the neck to the other, and the deepness of 2 1/8" deep is from throat to the back of neck. All the above measurement is made without padding. In other word, the exact measurement on the Bill Jee equipment.
Another thing I like to point out is the fact that for the top, the hood is covering over the head; however, for the bottom, the hood has to cover the neck inverted, in other word, bottom up.

                        Thank you once more for everything.

                              Thank you ever so much,

                                    Bruce

Dear George,

Masterful! Simply masterful! Dan and Linda are stunned when they see the Yin/Yang symbol. They said it's way better than the other "professional sign" given to me by Allen. Like I said previously it is very very artful.

Also, I must thank you for the name plates and the stainless steel card container — they are the greatest! My deep appreciation for your time and thoughtfulness.

First of all, I like you to mail me your membership card at your earliest convenience.

The drawing on the bottom, 1st page gives the exact measurement. In comparison to a human head, the width 7¼" is from ear to ear, the height 3⅞" is from forehead to top of nose, and the deepness of 1½" is from front of head to back of head. Now to the bottom part, the neck, as on a human. The "3⅛" is from underchin to bottom of neck above collar bone, the width 6⅝" is from the end of neck to the other, and the deepness of 2⅛" deep is from throat to the back of neck. All the above measurement is made without padding. In other word, the exact measurement on the 林 柱 equipment. Another thing I like to point out is the fact that for the top the hood is covering over the head; however, for the bottom, the hood has to cover the neck inverted, in other word, bottom up.

Thank you once more for everything. Thank you ever so much.

Bruce

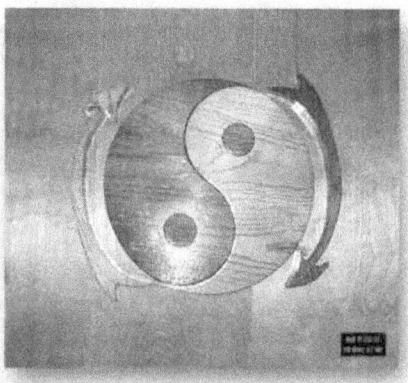

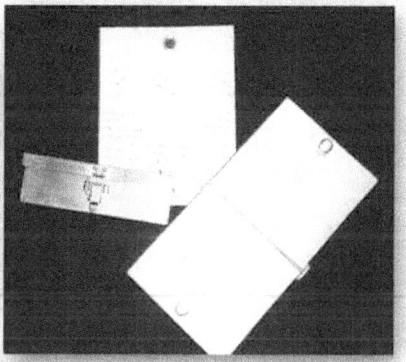

(top) Name plates made by George Lee for Bruce Lee as described in this letter.

(middle) Yin/Yang sign made by George Lee for Bruce Lee to be hung on Bruce's desk. Made 1967, this Yin/Yang sign detaches into many parts, a complicated masterpiece that Bruce cherished.

(bottom) Made by George Lee for Bruce Lee, these lock boxes and file containers were the start between Bruce and George and the long collaboration they had with building equipment.

Letter 5

Description of Letter No. 5

This letter brings back great memories for me. I remember going to see Bruce on the set of the "Green Hornet." At one point, Bruce made us part of the crew, and we participated in the shooting of a scene.
So there we were: James Lee, Allen Joe and me. To give the impression Bruce was driving down a street, the three of us bounced up and down on his car bumper while he pretended to be driving.
Later, Bruce took us over to see how "Batman and Robin" was shot. It was so funny to see Batman and Robin swinging from wires attached to the studio ceiling. When we were done there, we went to see how "Payton Place" was filmed. That was truly a wonderful day in my life.

Transcription

Dear George,

Just a letter to see how may favorite student is coming along – I'm sorry that I couldn't teach you as we planned because there is a slight change in the 20th Century Fox deal. Probably James Lee has told you about it; at any rate, the "Green Hornet" is going to be on the air this coming September. At present I'm taking acting lessons from a very well known Jeff Cory, the best drama coach here in Hollywood.

I'll be giving private lessons before the series starts. The prospective students are so far Steve McQueen, Paul Newman, James Gardner, Dan Gordon and Vic Damone. The fee will be around $25 an hour.

Understand you are going to start with James again. It's nice and you should stick with it and go as often as you can. James is really not a good teacher, and you know what I'm talking about. However, as for now, you can gain some knowledge from him. Keep asking questions and follow what I've told you that nite.

I'm developing fully and fully 5 Way of Attacking and even James doesn't know it. Next time when I see you I hope I'll have time to show you and teach you because George you've got what It takes and your attitude certainly deserves the best.

The "Green Hornet" will start shooting the end of May and I'll be busy like hell but the first chance I have I like to take a trip to Oakland and we should go out to dinner.

Take care my friend and drop me a line when you have time. By the way, unless you know him well. Do not give my address to the students. Thanks.

Take care,
Bruce

Dear George,
           March 31, 1966

Just a letter to see how my favorite student is coming along — I'm sorry that I couldn't teach you as we planned because there is a slight change in the 20th Century Fox deal. Probably James Lee has told you about it; at any rate, the "Green Hornet" is going to be on the air this coming September. At present I'm taking acting lesson from a very well known Jeff Cory, the best drama coach here in Hollywood.

I'll be giving private lesson before the Series starts. The prospective students are so far Steve McQueen, Paul Newman, James Gardner, Don Gordon, and Vic Damone. The fee will be around $25 an hour.

Understand you are going to start with James again. It's nice and you should stick with it and go as often as you can. James is really not a good teacher, and you know what I'm talking about. However, as for now, you can gain some knowledge from him. Keep asking questions and follow what I've told you that nite.

I'm developing fully and fully the 5 Way of Attacking and even James doesn't know it (due to his liquor & drinking). Next time when I see you I hope I'll have time to show you and teach you because George you've got what it takes and your attitude certainly deserve the best.

The "Green Hornet" will start shooting the end of May and I'll be busy like hell but the first chance I have I like to take a trip to Oakland and we should go out dinner.

Take care my friend and drop me a line when you have time. By the way, unless you know him well, do not give my address to the students. Thanks.

Bruce

Promotional still of Bruce Lee for "The Green Hornet", posing as a body builder, promoting his prowess.

Letter 6

Description of Letter No. 6

When I read this letter, it takes me back to the times I used to make Bruce different kinds of punching bags. They came in all sizes. Bruce truly liked the craftsmanship on the bags. They were durable, and he liked that.

Transcription

Dear George,

Thank you very much for those two punching bags!

Dan picked me up this morning and he will put one of the bag up on the wall in the gym today.

Well, tomorrow I'll take off again and it will be a long trip –

Again thank you for those bags, and as usual they are terrific.

                                        Bruce

See you this weekend.

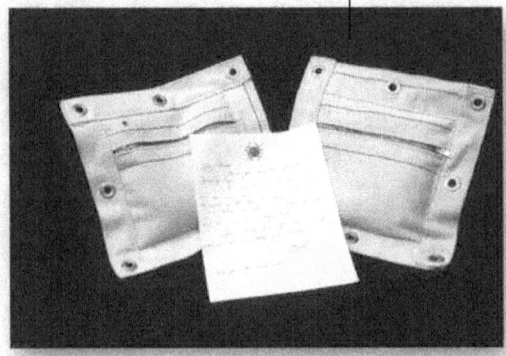

(above) As described in this letter, these are just a few of the punching pads George Lee made for Bruce Lee over the course of their close friendship.

(right) Bruce Lee standing side-by-side Dan Inosanto at the LA Chinatown School. George Lee's now famous Jeet Kune Do signs he collaborated on with Bruce, philosophically hanging on the wall in the background.

Dear George,

Thank you very much for those two punching bags!

Dan picked me up this morning and he will put one of the bag up on the wall in the gym to-day.

Well, to-morrow I'll take off again and it will be a long trip -------

Again thank you for those bags, and as usual they are terrific

Bruce

See you this week-end

Letter 7

Description of Letter No. 7

This letter really takes me back. I remember Bruce doing a demonstration on stage with James Lee. Bruce executed a technique, but James moved forward way too much. As a result, Bruce hit him with full force, making his nose bleed heavily. When it happened, the audience became dead silent and just stared at the two men on stage.

The accident occurred because James was off balance. James stumbled toward Bruce's punch and was hit. It was serious at that time, but now it is quite humorous.

In this letter, Bruce also mentioned a pair of shoes I made for him. He wanted a pair of shoes with a metal lining in between the sole and bottom of the shoe. This was really a hard job for me, but I finally was able to make them the way he liked it.

I asked Bruce what these shoes were for, and he told me the shoes were to kick people in the shins if they got too close. When he left the set of "The Green Hornet," people would grab him and ask for an autograph. He said someone once tore his shirt off and hurt him.

Bruce was truly a funny guy. It just shows you that he was constantly coming up with great ideas that revolved around his martial arts skill.

Transcription

Dear George,

I'm glad you made it to the luau. Allen Joe went too but he couldn't get in. Anyway, I'm glad it's over as I'm sick of demonstrations.

The two punching pad is out of sight and Dan flipped when he saw them. He said it's too beautiful to be used in class. We might as well know that whatever you make you turn it into a masterpiece.

Terrific.

There will be a birthday get together party at my house on Nov. 25, Sat. So let me know if you can make it for this weekend and come up on Friday nite (Nov.24). I'll send you a round trip ticket. So do let me know as soon as you can. Do not tell James or anyone I'm sending you the ticket though.

Again thank you for your "cool" equipment,

                                                         Bruce

P.S. The shoes are really nicely put together.

Bruce Lee with a fellow actor friend taking five on the set of "The Green Hornet".

Dear George,

I'm glad you made it to the luau. Allen Joe went too but he couldn't get in. Anyway, I'm glad it's over as I'm sick of demonstration.

The two punching pad is out of sight and Dan flipped when he saw them. He said it's too beauty to be used in class. We might as well know that whatever you make you turn is into a masterpiece. Terrific.

There will be a birthday get together party at my house on Nov. 25, Sat. So let me know if you can make it for this week-end and come up on Friday nite (Nov. 24). I'll send you a round trip ticket. So do let me know as soon as you can. Do not tell James or anyone I'm sending you the ticket though.

Again thank you for your "cool" equipment.

Bruce

P.S. The shoes are really nicely put together.

Letter 8

Description of Letter No. 8

Bruce's love for the grip machine that I made for him is what stands out in my mind about this letter. His forearms were incredible, and he always praised me for my work on this piece of equipment. To this day, when I see Bruce posing in a magazine or on film, his forearms always jump out at me.

Transcription

Dear George,

It was nice of you to call.

I'll probably come down one weekend in the middle of the next month to pick up some of the weights. By the way, the grip machine you made for me is darn good, and it helps me in my training very much. If and when I make the trip, I will let you know, as I like to get together with you.

Thanks again for your thoughtful call, and do drop me a line when you have the time.

Take care my friend.

Bruce

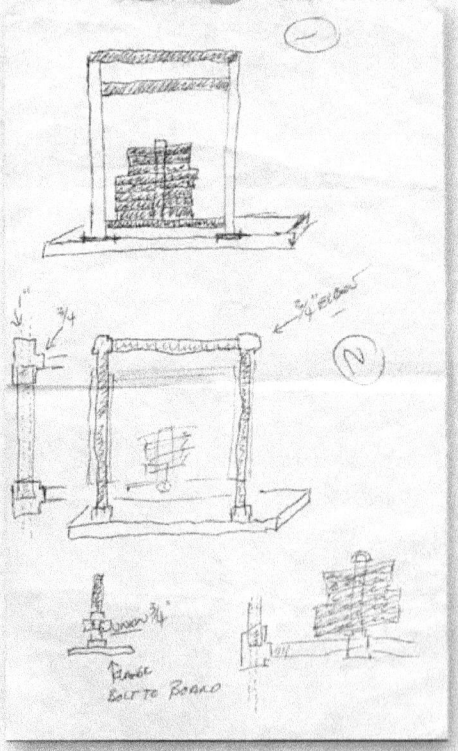

(below) The famous weight wrist grip machine that George Lee made for Bruce Lee. Bruce loved this machine and used it daily. This machine helped define all of Bruce's wrist and forearm muscles and gave him incredible strength.

(right) The original conception drawings for the now famous grip machine.

Dear George, June 25 1966

It was nice of you to call.

I'll probably come down one weekend in the middle of next month to pick up some of the weights. By the way, the grip machine you made for me is darn good, and it helps me in my training very much. If and when I make the trip, I will let you know, as I like to get together with you.

Thanks again for your thoughtful call, and do drop me a line when you have the time.

Take care my friend

Promotional head shot of Bruce Lee promoting the "Green Hornet".

Letter 9

Description of Letter No. 9

Once again, this is a letter in which Bruce mentioned the bags I made for him. Bruce used to hang the bags, which were all different sizes, everywhere.

I remember a bag I made for him that was very small. We were at dinner one night when he took out this bag and put it on the table. He then started doing finger jabs on it. Bruce was constantly training. He was one of a kind.

Transcription

George, the master maker,

Thanks for those four "magnificent" throwing Bags! Man, they are cool – really cool.

With appreciation,
Bruce

Bruce Lee showing at the beach his martial arts prowess, kicking high. Bruce Lee often was the center of the camera lens, documenting his journey through his martial arts growth.

George, the master maker,

    Thanks for those four "magnificent" throwing tags! Man, they are cool — really cool.

                  With appreciation

                  Bruce

Letter 10

Description of Letter No. 10

I remember making many different types of kicking and punching shields for Bruce. I used to enjoy making them.

Bruce also mentioned in this letter that he and James Coburn were working on a project that was supposed to be called "The Silent Flute." Bruce was truly excited about doing this, and he looked forward to working with Coburn.

I can remember Bruce telling me one of the parts he was going to play was a wise blind man. Bruce actually had contact lenses made up for the role. He was very close to doing that project, and it would have been a great one.

Transcription

Dear George,

After experimenting on the shield, we find that because of the thickness and extra weight, it absorbs The shock much better. Therefore the holder is not as miserable as before, thanks to you.

As I mentioned, we are preparing a script, Coburn, Silliphant and I. Coburn and I will star in it. We hope to start shooting the end of the year, if Coburn's schedule is opened. If not, then it has to be next march. At any rate, this will be the start of something really really big for me.

Take care my friend and thank you once more,

Bruce

(left) Bruce Lee in pose, throwing a kick for the camera as James Coburn snaps the shot, in India, location scouting for Bruce Lee's Silent Flute project that never came to light.

(right) The punching and kicking shield George Lee made for Bruce Lee as stated in this letter. Bruce Lee used this shield as an intricate part of his martial arts training, especially in the early days. He loved this piece of equipment.

George,

    After experimenting on the shield, we find that because of the thickness and extra weight, it absorbs the shock much better. Therefore the holder is not as miserable as before, thanks to you.

    As I mentioned, we are preparing a script, Coburn, Silliphant and I. Coburn and I will star in it. We hope to start shooting the end of the year, if Coburn's schedule is opened. If not, then it has to be next March. At any rate, this will be the start of something really really big for me.

    Take care my friend and thank you once more

Bruce

Letter 11

Description of Letter No. 11

I liked James Coburn as an actor, and I asked Bruce to get me an autographed picture from him. Bruce eventually sent me a signed photo from James, and it was great to get something like that from such a big movie star.

Transcription

Dear George,

A letter to let you know that Coburn's picture should be on its way next week. I just returned from The East Coast with him. McQueen is in Europe, so his has to wait. Just want to let you know I haven't forgotten my friend.

My mother and brother are here. They are presently staying with me.

Things are going great with me – will let you know when they develop.

Take care,

Bruce

(left) A thank you letter from James Coburn sent to George Lee for making him punching bags. James Coburn felt George Lee was a true artist.

(right) An autograph picture from James Coburn to George Lee. George often made equipment for Bruce's celebrity friends upon request.

George,

    A letter to let you know that Coburn's picture should be on its way next week. I just returned from the East Coast with him. McQueen is in Europe, so he has to wait. Just want to let you know I haven't forgotten my friend.

    My mother and brother are here. They are presently staying with me.

    Things are going great with me — will let you know when they develop.

    Take Care,

    Bruce

Letter 12

Description of Letter No. 12

This letter is just another example of the appreciation Bruce showed to me for making equipment for him.

Transcription

Dear George,

Finally moved but still unpacking and a lot of rearranging. It's a hell of a job but I must take time out to once more thank you for that magnificent job you did on that finger jab equipment. I've already heard from James that the base for the leg stretcher will be terrific. Actually, I need not have him to inform me on that. Man, like everything you touch has to be beautiful or else you won't deliver it.

I'm flying up this weekend, give me a call at James and we'll get together. I will sharpen at least one of your technique with my newly found training method. Okay, George.

Take care my friend,
Bruce

 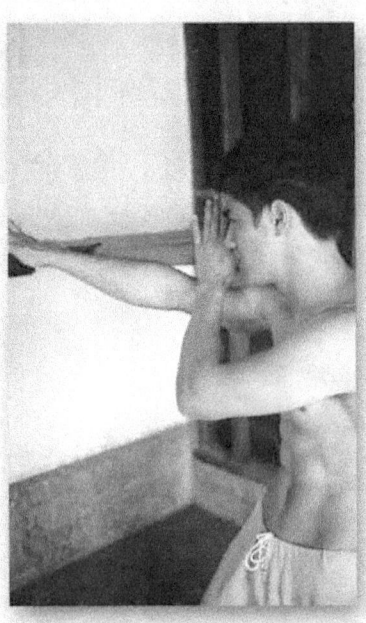

(left) Bruce Lee stretching on the now famous leg stretcher machine George Lee made for Bruce Lee as stated in this letter. Bruce Lee used this piece of equipment on a daily basis.

(right) Bruce Lee doing a "Bill Jee" technique on a piece of equipment George Lee made for him as stated in this letter. Bruce's skills with his hands were unmatched and machines such as these helped him honed his skill.

George,

    Finally moved but still unpacking and a lot of rearranging. It's a hell of a job but I must take time out to once more thank you for that magnificent job you did on that finger jab equipment. I've already heard from James that the base for the leg stretcher will be terrific. Actually I need not have him to inform me on that. Man, like everything you touch has to be beautiful or else you won't deliver it.

    I'm flying up this week-end, give me a call at James and we'll get together. I will sharpen at least one of your technique with my newly found training method. Okay. George

    Take Care my friend

    Bruce

Letter 13

Description of Letter No. 13

In this letter from Bruce, he expressed how he liked the kicking and punching equipment I made for him. Bruce was always asking me to make more of this type of equipment because he beat up the boards pretty good. Therefore, he always needed me to make more for him. Furthermore, his friends also wanted boards. Bruce also mentioned a film project that he was working on with Steve McQueen. I never heard what happened to this project, but I know Bruce was excited about it.

Transcription

Dear George,

Remember the kicking and punching padded boards you made for me – well, after using them for a while, I have come to many improvements. When you have the time, can you make an extra kicking board and punching board for me? Your kicking board is top for kicking, no heavy bag can replace it. The accompany sheets will describe the added improvements.

Steve McQueen, after he completes his movie in Frisco, will get a writer and start on a Gung Fu movie with him and I in it. So this is a start toward the movie.

On April 6 I probably will come up because there is a so called "National Gung Fu Exhibition," held in Frisco – a bunch of jerks will be in there, including Chris Chan, the president by the way, and the runner Wong Jack Man. I will show up to scare hell out of them.

Take care,
Bruce

How do you like new cards – am teaching a few guys private lessons now.

Bruce Lee in pose, standing next to James Lee, Brandon picture right. Bruce holding the now famous Tombstone in dramatic pose, symbolizing the philosophical meaning of the equipment made for him by George Lee. James Lee holding the now famous kicking shield made for Bruce.

George,

Remember the kicking and punching padded boards you made for me — well, after using them for a while, I have come to many improvements. When you have time, can you make an extra kicking board and punching board for me? Your kicking board is top for kicking; no heavy bag can replace it. The accompany sheets will describe the added improvements.

Steve McQueen, after he completes his movie in Frisco, will get a writer and start on a Gung Fu movie with him and I in it. So this is a start toward the movie.

On April 6 I probably will come up because there is a so called "National Gung Fu Exhibition" held in Frisco — a bunch of jerks will be in there, including Chris Chan, the President by the way, and the runner 黃仁智 — I will show up to scare hell out of them.

Take Care

Bruce

How do you like new cards — am teaching a few guys private lessons now.

Letter 14

Description of Letter No. 14

This is another letter in which Bruce talked about some of the things I made for him. It made me feel good when Bruce told me how he and others appreciated what I created.

Transcription

Dear George,

It was nice seeing you in Oakland and thanks again for that "beautiful" stained and "cool" pins you made for me. Ted Wong thinks you are the greatest craftman.

The two handles you made for the finger bowl do not fit as the four holes on the side of the bowl do not match the screws on the handles. I imagine it's rather difficult when the bowl is already here in L.A. Enclosed are the positions of the four holes on each side of the finger bowl.

When you can find the time (any time from now) do drop me a line so that I can send you a plane ticket to come down during week-end. I'm sure I can sharpen your Gung Fu techniques during this period. Of course at the same time you can look over my desk.

I'll be working on my book once again now that I'm settled down and those photos you were in look great.

Take care my friend.

With Appreciation,

Bruce

(left) Bruce about to throw one of his lethal kicks in his apartment at the Barrington Plaza complex off of Wilshire Blvd Los Angeles.

(right) These Jeet Kune Do class pins and key chains were made by George Lee for Bruce Lee and were also given out to the higher-level students of the Oakland school.

George,

    It was nice seeing you in Oakland and thanks again for that "beautiful" skinned and "cool" pins you made for me. Ted Wong thinks you are the greatest craftman.

    The two handles you made for the finger bowl do not fit as the four holes on the side of the bowl do not match the screws on the handles. I imagine it's rather difficult when the bowl is already here in L.A. Enclosed are the positions of the four hole on each side of the finger bowl.

    When you can find time (any time from now) do drop me a line so that I can send you a plane ticket to come down during a week-end. I'm sure I can sharpen your Gung fu techniques during the period. Of course at the same time you can look over my desk.

    I'll be working on my book once again now that I'm settled down and those photos you were in look great.

    Take care my friend

with appreciation

Bruce

Letter 15

Description of Letter No. 15

This is a letter from Bruce in which he informed me that he was coming to Oakland and wanted to get together so we could train. My training sessions with Bruce incorporated physical training and philosophy. Those times were truly great.

Transcription

Dear George,

I am coming to Oakland on May 26, this coming Friday at around 5 P.M. and will go to James Freemont class for a short lecture-type lesson for his students. Then I would like to get together with you, James and Allen for a Gung Fu session (probably next day, Sat.) However, if you can go to the Fremont class with us you can come and leave your car at James. I think you do know some of the students there.

At any rate, hope to see you this trip, and that nothing sudden comes up to prevent me from coming.

Take care,

Bruce

Bruce Lee in punching pose for an interview conducted by "Black Belt" magazine in 1966.

George,

    I am coming to Oakland on May 26, this coming Friday at around 5 P.M. and will go to James for Fremont class for a short lecture-type lesson for his students. Then I would like to get together with you, James and Allen for a Gung Fu session (probably next day, Sat.) However, if you can go to the Fremont class with us you can come and leave your car at James. I think you do know some of the students there.

    At any rate, hope to see you this trip, and that nothing sudden comes up to prevent me from coming.

    Take Care.

                                Bruce

Letter 16

Description of Letter No. 16

Here is a letter that showed Bruce's concern for my well-being. Bruce was a giving friend and he truly cared about others.

Transcription

Dear George,

I heard from James that you didn't feel good. I hope you're much better by now.

                                      Take care,

                                        Bruce

Bruce Lee kicking high in traditional gung fu style in this promotional picture showing Bruce as the "Kung Fu Master", taken in 1966.

George,

    I heard from James that you didn't feel good. I hope you're much better by now.

    Take care my friend

                        Bruce

Letter 17

Description of Letter No. 17

I remember when Bruce and I would go out to eat and discuss the martial arts and philosophy. Those times were great.

Transcription

Dear George,

Will be coming up to Oakland this coming Friday (Feb. 16).

Take care,
Bruce

Bruce Lee at a "Black Belt Magazine" gathering, Robert Wall and Chuck Norris look on, as Bruce becomes the center of attention. Photo taken end of 1967.

George,

Will be coming up to Oakland this coming Friday (Feb. 16).
See you then

Bruce

Letter 18

Description of Letter No. 18

This is another letter about equipment and different events that surrounded Bruce's life.

Transcription

Dear George,

Enclosed please find the pins of our school.

It was nice seeing you during my visit and you looked well as usual.

One idea for the long bag (for kicking) is to make it like the regular punch bag that you made with punched holes on both sides. That way I can lower or make it higher

When Linda came to pick me up the car had an accident – lucky nobody got hurt. Brandon bumped his head slightly. The car is out for a few days.

Take care,
Bruce

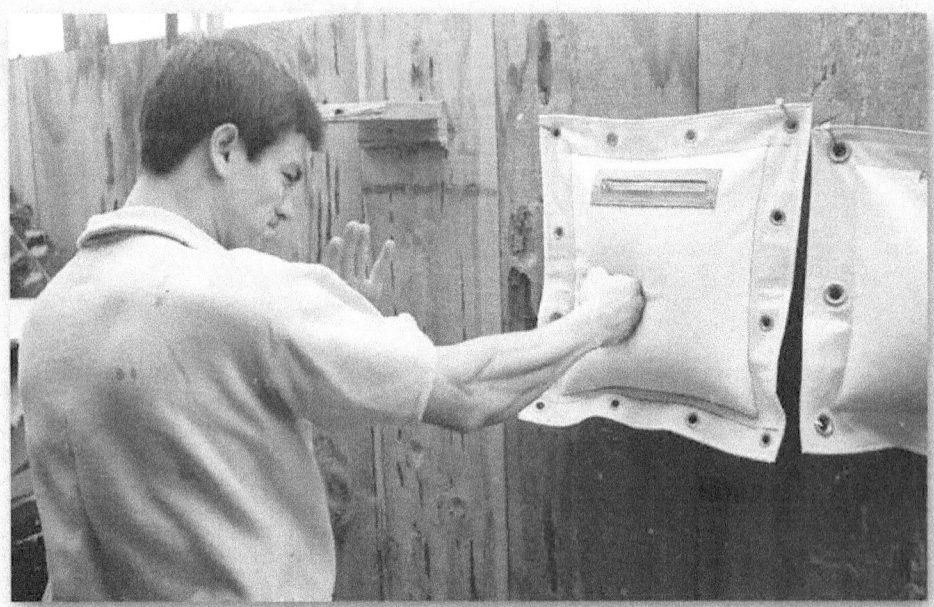

Bruce Lee in punching form, striking bags that George Lee made for him. Bruce in his backyard in Culver City.

George,

Enclosed please find the pins of our school.

It was nice seeing you during my visit and you looked well as usual.

One idea for the long bag (for kicking) is to make it like the regular punch bag that you made with punched holes on both sides. That way I can lower or make it higher

When Linda came to pick me up the car had an accident — lucky nobody got hurt. Brandon bumped his head slightly. The car is out for a few days

Take Care

Bruce

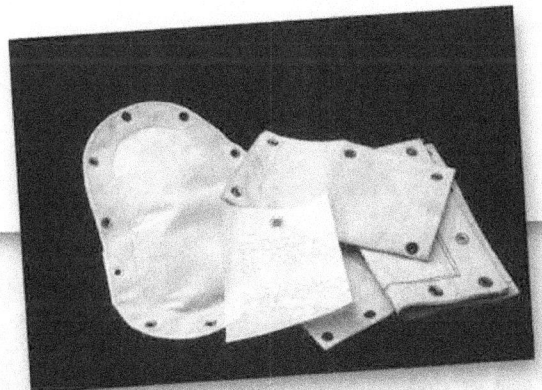

Special punching bags made for Bruce Lee. In this letter, Bruce describes in how he prefers the bags to be made to help further his progress within his training.

Letter 19

Description of Letter No. 19

This letter means a lot to me because Bruce told me that he considered me a close friend. I never heard Bruce say this to many others, so I took it to heart. This letter made me feel pretty good.

Transcription

Dear George,

I tried like hell, but I just can't get away during the Thanksgiving week-end. I would very much like to come because you're one of my very close friends. I want you to know that.

As soon as I have things clear here – (I've been very busy working) – I would come up and give you a call.

By the way, James Coburn ("Our Man Flint") would like to have one of your wall bags. Can you get him one?

Will talk to you soon.

Thank you again for your kind invitation,

Bruce

Bruce in stoic pose looking sharp for the camera. I remember Bruce always looking cool and when we went places, people always noticed him; he seemed to always have that special aura about him.

George,

    I tried like hell, but I just can't get away during the Thanksgiving week-end. I would very much like to come because you're one of my very close friend I want you to know that.

    As soon as I have things clear here — (I've been very busy working) — I would come up and give you a call.

    By the way, James Coburn ("Our man Flint") would like to have one of your wall bag. Can you get him one?

    Will talk to you soon
    Thank you again for your kind invitation

Bruce

Letter 20

Description of Letter No. 20

What stands out most of all in this letter is Bruce's reference to his workout program. As you can see, Bruce truly worked hard on getting himself into great shape. Many people look at Bruce in magazines or movies and do not realize the work he put in to get into that great shape. Not only was Bruce a well-rounded martial artist, he also lifted weights.

Transcription

Dear George,

Haven't written for a little while, how are things?

Your wall punching bags have definitely helped in my daily training. I've started the training on Christmas eve. My 1968 resolution. I now train an average of 2 1/2 hrs. a day, including hand exercises, leg exercises, running, isometric, stomach exercises, sparring exercises, free hand exercises. Your training equipments all help in my program. Thanks.

Allen Joe must have told you about James Lee's surprise party on Jan 26 (Friday nite) – I'll fly in that nite without letting him know. Do your best to be there; after all, you are one of the very important members.

So take care my friend, and my best to your wife and family.

Bruce

By the way, could you give me your home phone number once more?

Bruce Lee exchanging information with George Dillman. Bruce traveled to the East Coast on more than one occasion, showing up at martial arts events to promote himself, also helping the people putting on the event get a good turnout. People always loved coming to see Bruce, he had that great energy about him.

George,

Haven't written for a little while, how are things?

Your wall punching bags have definitely helped in my daily training. I've started the training on Christmas Eve, my 1968 resolution. I now train an average of 2½ hrs. a day, including hand exercises, leg exercise, running, isometric, stomach exercise, spar exercises, free hand exercises. Your training equipments all help in my program. Thanks.

Allen Joe must have told you about James Lee's surprise party on Jan 26 (Friday nite) — I'll fly in that nite without letting him know. Do your best to be there; after all, you are one of the very important member.

So take care my friend, and my best to your wife and family.

Bruce

By the way, could you give me your home phone number once more —

Made by George Lee, this isometric machine helped develop Bruce Lee's arms as well as his upper back and helped strengthened his stomach as well. This machine was a holistic approach to help develop through tension, exercising his complete form. He loved this machine.

Letter 21

Description of Letter No. 21

Bruce kept in touch to let me know about projects he had in the works. Bruce used to travel a lot, and he did many shows and exhibitions. I remember he was always working on something.

Transcription

Dear George,

I still feel bad about that mixed up date. I thought it was Sept 29 (Sunday).

I'll be leaving for Mississippi with Steve. The project on Jeet Kune Do as a movie is taking another step. Stirling Silliphant (In The Heat of The Nite) is involved to write the script. We will be getting together and roll. After that I'll be flying to New York a few days.

Of course in the midst of all these I'm moving too. As of next Monday, my new address will be:

> 2551 Roscomare Rd.
> Los Angeles, Calif. 90024

It's a pretty "cool" house located inside Bel Air. As soon as I have the phone in, I'll let you know. Anyway, let me know if you can come down in Nov. 27. Maybe we should arrange it at a different date. At any rate, the next day will be Thanksgiving.

Take care my friend,
Bruce

Bruce Lee sits along side Stirling Silliphant discussing "The Silent Flute" idea. Bruce taught many celebrity students in Hollywood, and Stirling was a student who liked my training equipment, especially the kicking shield.

George,

I still feel bad about that mixed up date. I thought it was Sept 29 (Sunday).

I'll be leaving for Mississippi with Steve. The project on Jeet Kune Do as a movie is taking another step. Sterling Silliphant (In the Heat of the Nite) is involved to write the script. We will be getting together and roll. After that I'll be flying to New York for a few days.

Of course in the midst of all these I'm moving too. As of next Monday, my address will be

2551 Roscomare Rd.
Los Angeles, Calif. 90024.

It's a pretty "cool" house located inside Bel-Air. As soon as I have the phone in, I'll let you know.

Anyway, let me know if you can come down in Nov. 27. Maybe we should arrange it at a different date. At any rate, the next day will be Thanksgiving.

Take care my friend

Bruce

Letter 22 — page 1

Description of Letter No. 22 (page 1)

In this letter, Bruce praised me for making more equipment for him. He also drew a diagram of headgear that he wanted me to make. Bruce was a great artist, and he loved to draw.

Transcription (page 1)

Dec. 18 1965

Dear George,

It was nice to see you when I was down in Oakland. Of all the students I like you the most. You got what it takes.

I must thank you once more for the grip machine (not to mention the dip bar, the name plate and others –). When you make something it's always professional like.

My gripping power and forearm have improved greatly – thanks for your wrist roller.

Understand that Dave Young has quit the class – anyway, that guy just doesn't have the right attitude.

Linda and I will be coming down to Oakland to stay for around a month before either going to Hollywood or Hong Kong. The 20th Century Fox deal is 85%. If that doesn't come out I have two contracts waiting in Hong Kong.

During this coming one month stay I want you to drop by at least once a week at the house. Because I want to show you all the Gung Fu techniques. I know you will benefit greatly from these instructions and I trust you will not show it to other students.

The wrist roller machine I made for Bruce Lee helped him greatly in strengthening his forearms. He loved this machine and used it daily. He could do this for hours if he wanted too, he couldn't get enough of it.

George,　　　　　　　Dec. 18 1965

It was nice to see you when I was down in Oakland. Of all the students I like you the most. You got what it takes.

I must thank you once more for the grip machine (not to mention the dip bar, the name plate and others ---). When you make something it's always professional like.

My gripping power and forearm have improved greatly —— thanks for your Wrist Roller.

Understand that Dave Young has quit the class — anyway, that joker just doesn't have the right attitude.

Linda and I will be coming down to Oakland to stay for around a month before either going to Hollywood or Hong Kong. The 20th Century Fox deal is 85%. If that doesn't come out I have two contracts waiting in Hong Kong.

Letter 22 page 2

Description of Letter No. 22 (page 2)

In this letter, Bruce praised me for making more equipment for him. He also drew a diagram of headgear that he wanted me to make. Bruce was a great artist, and he loved to draw.

Transcription (page 2)

I'm drawing the following diagrams to show you how a naval head-guard looks like.

Front view   Side View

The protective equipment is the most important invention in Gung Fu. It WILL raise the standard of Gung Fu to unbelievable height. In order for Gung Fu to remain supreme over the other systems the protective equipment is a must. With the ability you have in making things, I have confidence in your building the first practical protective equipment in the history of Gung Fu. Your work will be remembered. Gung Fu NEEDS it. I've written James to tell him to help you in every way he can. If you need any help call him. Start with this great plan at your earliest convenience and devote whatever time you have. This plan depends on YOU because knowing the rest of the guys, they do not have the incentive or the ability. James should be able to help you some.

Take care of yourself my friend,

Bruce Lee

Bruce Lee doing a demonstration with Daniel Inosanto in Los Angeles, California.

During this coming one month stay I want you to drop by at least once a week at the house. Because I want to show you all the Gung Fu techniques. I know you will benefit greatly from these instructions and I trust you will not show it to other students.

I'm ~~ever~~ drawing the following diagrams to show you how a naval head-guard looks like.

FRONT VIEW   SIDE VIEW

The protective equipment is *the* most important in Gung Fu. It will set the standard of Gung Fu to unbelievable height. In order for Gung Fu to remain supreme over the other [arts]

the protective equipment is a must. With the ability you have in making things, I have confidence in your building the first practical protective equipment in the history of Gung Fu. Your work will be remembered. Gung Fu NEEDS it.

I've written James to tell him to help you in every way he can. If you need any help call him. Start with this great plan at your earliest convenience and devote whatever time you have. This plan depends on YOU because knowing the rest of the guys, they do not have the incentive or the ability. James should be able to help you some.

Take care of yourself
my friend

Bruce Lee

Letter 23 — page 1

Description of Letter No. 23

This letter brings back some great memories. Among other things, Bruce talked about filming "Batman."
Of course, we all know by now that Bruce did the "Green Hornet." One of the shows featured the "Green Hornet" meets "Batman and Robin." Bruce had many stories to tell about this. I will just say this. Bruce was the better fighter.
Next, Bruce drew some diagrams that he wanted me to make into signs. These signs, which show the path one takes in Bruce's system, became famous after his passing. Bruce felt that these illustrations were very important to show people the philosophy behind the art. There is also a diagram of a tombstone, which illustrates how one can be swallowed up by the classical mess of the so-called many kung-fu styles. This also became famous after Bruce's passing.

Transcription (page 1)

Dear George,

I've been shooting Batman these few days and busy like hell. I believe I should be able to find time to show your boy and his friends around the studio this coming Friday.

The Oklahoma appearance was great and I'm asked back for another one in Georgia. That sign you made has created quite a hit – everyone admires your talents.

If you have time, I like to make two requests for some stuffs that you can make for me. They are gadgets to put my system across.

First, I like three signs for hanging like pictures on wall – slightly smaller than the sign you made for me. Here are the plans & ideas – this project by the way is to illustrate the thought behind my system – the 3 stages

Explanation for the three signs (same black shining background as the sign you made)

FIRST SIGN

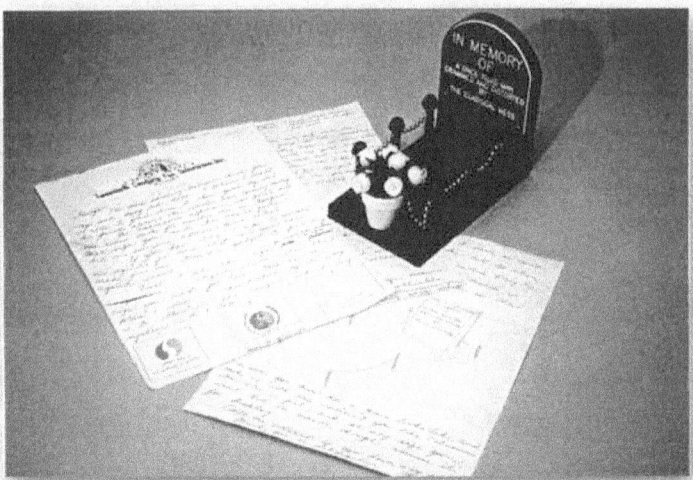

The Tombstone I made for Bruce Lee was originally conceived by him. He wanted something he could put on his desk for people to see in regards to his belief that the not too alive way of the classical Kung Fu styles can inhibit your growth as a martial artist, a kind of sarcasm on his behalf that has a valuable lesson within.

Twentieth Century-Fox Television, Inc.
BOX 900
BEVERLY HILLS CALIFORNIA

George,

I've been shooting Batman these few days and busy like hell. I believe I should be able to find time to show your toy and his friends around the studio this coming Friday.

The Oklahoma appearance was great and I'm asked back for another one in Georgia. That sign you made has created quite a hit — everyone admires your talent.

If you have time, I like to make two requests for some stuffs that you can make for me. They are gadgets to put my system across.

First, I like three signs for hanging like picture on wall — slightly smaller than the sign you made for me. Here are the plans & ideas — this project by the way is to illustrate the thought behind my system — the 3 stages

1. PARTIALITY — THE RUNNING TO EXTREME
2. FLUIDITY — THE TWO HALVES OF ONE WHOLE
3. EMPTINESS — THE FORMLESS FORM

Turn to next

A picture of the classical mess tombstone in Bruce Lee's backyard in Culver City, California. He loved this creation and kept it on his desk both in Los Angeles and Hong Kong where he became an international movie star.

Letter 23 page 2

Description of Letter No. 23

This letter brings back some great memories. Among other things, Bruce talked about filming "Batman."

Of course, we all know by now that Bruce did the "Green Hornet." One of the shows featured the "Green Hornet" meets "Batman and Robin." Bruce had many stories to tell about this. I will just say this. Bruce was the better fighter.

Next, Bruce drew some diagrams that he wanted me to make into signs. These signs, which show the path one takes in Bruce's system, became famous after his passing. Bruce felt that these illustrations were very important to show people the philosophy behind the art. There is also a diagram of a tombstone, which illustrates how one can be swallowed up by the classical mess of the so-called many kung-fu styles. This also became famous after Bruce's passing.

Transcription (page 2)

here all we need is one red half and one gold half of the yin yang symbol. HOWEVER no dot is need on either halves; in other word it is just plain red with no gold dot, or just plain gold with no red dot (this serves to illustrate extreme softness (like Tygik) or/ and extreme hardness (like Hung Gar). So just follow the drawing and also put the phrase – PARTIALITY – THE RUNNING TO EXTREME on the black board.

SECOND SIGN

Exact yin yang symbol like the sign you made for me except there is no Chinese characters around the symbol. Of course, the phrase – FLUIDITY – THE TWO HLVES OF ONE WHOLE will be on the black board.

THIRD SIGN

Just a shinny black board with nothing on it except the phrase EMPTINESS – THE FORMLESS FORM.

The three signs have to be the same size because they illustrate the three stages of cultivation.

Bruce Lee practicing Bill Jee, or finger jabs in this metal engraved pot I made him, hitting metal BB's. Bruce was a true innovator within the training world; he did things no one else thought of at that time. He was 50 years ahead of his time.

Explanation for the three signs (same black shining background as the sign you made)

FIRST SIGN

here all we need is one red half and one gold half of the Yin Yang symbol. HOWEVER <u>no</u> dot is need on either halves; in other word it is just plain red with no gold dot, or just plain gold with no red dot (this serves to illustrate extreme softness (like 太極拳) or /and extreme hardness (like 洪家). So just follow the drawing and also put the phrase — PARTIALITY — THE RUNNING TO EXTREME on the black board

SECOND SIGN

Exact yin yang symbol like the sign you made for me except there is <u>no</u> chinese Characters around the symbol. Of course, the phrase — FLUIDITY — THE TWO HALVES OF ONE WHOLE will be on the black board.

THIRD SIGN

Just a shinny black board with nothing on it except the phrase EMPTINESS — THE FORMLESS FORM.

the three signs have to be the same size because they illustrate the three stages of cultivation. Please do make them like the sign you made for me aluminum and symbol and shinny black board

Letter 23 page 3

Description of Letter No. 23

This letter brings back some great memories. Among other things, Bruce talked about filming "Batman."
Of course, we all know by now that Bruce did the "Green Hornet." One of the shows featured the "Green Hornet" meets "Batman and Robin." Bruce had many stories to tell about this. I will just say this. Bruce was the better fighter.
Next, Bruce drew some diagrams that he wanted me to make into signs. These signs, which show the path one takes in Bruce's system, became famous after his passing. Bruce felt that these illustrations were very important to show people the philosophy behind the art. There is also a diagram of a tombstone, which illustrates how one can be swallowed up by the classical mess of the so-called many kung-fu styles. This also became famous after Bruce's passing.

Transcription (page 3)

Please do make them like the sign you made for me aluminum symbol and shinny black boards.

The second gadget I have in mind is used to dramatize the not too alive way of the classical so called Kung Fu styles. What I have in mind is a miniature "tomb stone" and here is the drawing

I'm sure you know how a grave looks like and make it with any material you like (aluminum tomb stone is fine) and at any size you want. NOT too small though, because it's for display.

Call me collect if you have any problem.

Thank you in anticipation,

Bruce

The original Yin Yang Jeet Kune Do conception drawings handed over to me by Bruce. A lot when into making these boards and Bruce loved the result. He hung them hi and proud at the Chinatown Gung Fu School in Los Angeles.

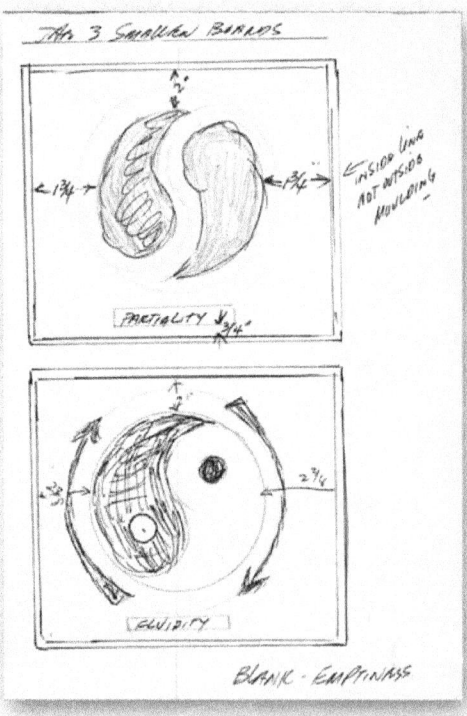

The second gadget I have in mind is used to dramatize the not too alive way of the Classical so called Kung Fu styles. What I have in mind is a miniature "tomb stone" and here is the drawing

I'm sure you know how a grave looks like and make it with any material you like (aluminum tomb stone is fine) and at any size you want. Not too small though, because it's for display.

Call me collect if you have any problem. Thank you in anticipation Bruce

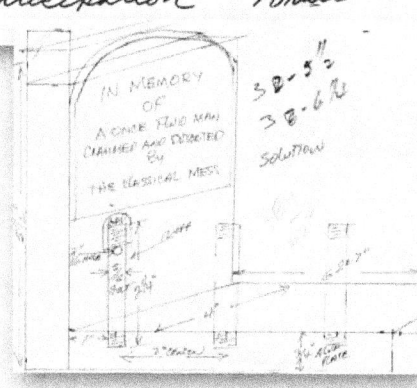

The original conception plans for the classical mess tombstone I built for Bruce Lee.

Letter 24

Description of Letter No. 24

In this letter, Bruce thanked me for sending padding for a shield. Bruce always shared his gratitude with me and treated me like a big brother.

Transcription

George,

A personal letter to thank you for your immediate sending of the padding. Also, I've given that punching pad to Delgado and he expressed his appreciation. As soon as I get around to give him your address, he would like to write to thank you.

So my friend have a Merry Christmas and definitely a rewarding New Year.

Again thank you kindly.

Take care,
Bruce

Bruce with Linda and Brandon relaxing up North at Luis Delgado's house. Though Bruce was a busy man seeking international fame, he always made time for his family. Linda and the kids were the true love of his life.

George,

    A personal letter to thank you for your immediate sending of the padding. Also, I've given that punching pad to Delgado and he expressed his appreciation. As soon as I get around to give him your address, he would like to write to thank you.

    So my friend have a merry Christmas and definitely a rewarding new year.

    Again thank you kindly

Warm Regards,

Bruce

Letter 25

Description of Letter No. 25

This letter reminds me that Bruce was not the only one who used the equipment that I made for him. Many others liked it, too, and many times Bruce would have me make equipment for other people, like Danny Inosanto. Even though I did not live in Los Angeles at that time, I feel we were all family sharing something special.

Transcription

Dear George,

Too bad you aren't here. You should have heard comments from the fellows down here! "Is he a pro artist." "I don't believe this!" (Dan said that) and many many more on the fine work you've created. As for me, they are terrific!! Thanks once more for the many hours you've put in; you're the greatest.

Bruce

Four pair of nunchaku I made for Bruce Lee. It took a lot of fine-tuning with these pieces of equipment. These were much more developed at that time than the ones in the marketplace. Bruce wanted the chains longer and the wood base handles were heavier for better stability. The weight with the chains were a factor as well. In the end, we came up with some memorable equipment he uses in his films, he loved them. I remember, Danny Inosanto originally showed Bruce how to use them and a week later, Bruce was showing Danny how to use them, Bruce was that good.

Dear George,

    Too bad you aren't here. You should have heard comments from the fellows down here! "Is he a pro artist" "I don't believe this!" (Dan said that) and many many more on the fine work you've created. As for me, they are terrific!! Thanks once more for the many hours you've put in; you're the greatest.

                        Bruce

Letter 26

Description of Letter No. 26

In this letter, Bruce commented on some equipment I made for him. Bruce and I had a close friendship, and we shared many ideas, which made many incredible memories.

Transcription

Dear George,

A masterpiece indeed! My appreciation my friend – not only to the workmanship (that is always top!) but particularly to your thoughtfulness.

Thank you George.

Peace – Love – Brotherhood,

Bruce

(right) Bruce Lee posing in traditional Chinese style costume. This was a test shoot with Bruce Lee for a film project he was supposed to do after filming "Enter the Dragon". He told me he needed me to make him an ancient Chinese axe he was to pose with and use in the film. I made the axe for him, but unfortunately, he passed away before he could receive the piece. He would have loved it.

(opposite page) This is the axe I made fro Bruce Lee, supposed to be used in a film he was about to do, but unfortunately, he passed away. Bruce's plans for this film were going to make it a blockbuster on many levels.

George,

A masterpiece indeed! My appreciation my friend —— not only to the workmanship (that is always top!) but particularly to your thoughtfulness. Thank you George

Peace – Love – Brotherhood

Bruce

Letter 27

Description of Letter No. 27

Bruce touched base with me to let me know what he was doing. Letters like this bring back memories of the simple times he and I shared.

Transcription

Dear George,

I'm coming to Oakland this coming Monday nite around 9:30 P.M. I'll probably give you a call.

I'll stay till Thursday afternoon and then will take off to New York for an appearance at the All American Open Karate Championship. I'll stay there for four days then I'll go to Seattle for a few days and then will come back to Oakland for a couple of days before I'll take off to Springfield, Mass. for another appearance.

Plan on coming down for the photo-shooting on the weekend of July 8.

Will talk to you when I see you.

Bruce

Bruce Lee preparing for a demonstration at the Long Beach Internationals that Ed Parker put on yearly. Bruce about to show his martial arts skills while blindfolded.

George,

    I'm coming to Oakland this coming Monday nite around 9:30 P.M. I'll probably give you a call.

    I'll stay till Thursday afternoon and then will take off to New York for an appearance at the All American Open Karate Championship. I'll stay there for four days then I'll go to Seattle for a few days and then will come back to Oakland for a couple of days before I'll take off to Springfield, Mass. for another appearance.

    Plan on coming down for the photo-shooting on the week-end of July 8.

    Will talk to you when I see you.

                          Bruce

Letters of Appreciation

Letter from *Linda Lee*

Linda Lee at James Lee's house relaxing in the backyard. Linda was Bruce's stone so to speak, he trusted her deeply and she was the perfect wife for him.

March 22, 1969

Dear George,

    Many thanks for remembering me on my birthday. You are always so thoughtful. We are in the final stages of preparation for our next-born now. As the time grows shorter I can think of so many things to do.

    Bruce has enjoyed the equipment you have made for him and they are such a big aid in teaching. You are truly a master craftman.

    If you plan to visit this way anytime, be sure to let us know. My regards to your wife.

                                 Sincerely,

                                   Linda

MRS. BRUCE LEE
2551 ROSCOMARE ROAD, LOS ANGELES, CALIFORNIA 90024

Mr. George Lee
1621 Zinn St.
Richmond, Calif. 94805

Letter from Steve McQueen

Bruce Lee center, Steve McQueen picture left and Fumio Demura right at a Los Angeles Karate demonstration. Steve McQueen was one of Bruce's students for a period of time, they both had this playful banter that went back and forth to who was the coolest guy. I made a few bags for Steve, he really liked that they could take a beating.

FROM STEVE McQUEEN

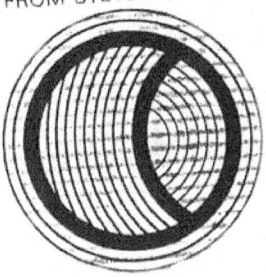

Thank you very much for the
green bean bag.

Steve McQueen

Steve McQueen
SOLAR PRODUCTIONS INC

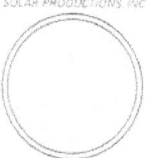

Mr. George Lee
1621 Zinn Street
Richmond, California 91405

Mr. George Lee
1621 Zinn Street
Richmond, Calif. 94805

Mr. George S. Lee
1621 Zinn Street
Richmond, Calif. 94805

Bruce Lee
2332 - 11th E
Seattle, Wash. 98102

Mr. George S. Lee
1621 Zinn Street
Richmond, Calif. 94805

Mr. George Lee
1621 Zinn Street
Richmond, Calif.

ALWAYS USE ZIP CODE

Rd.
Cal. 90024

George Lee

Practicing with a student

In these series of pictures a very young 48-year-old George Lee in 1965 exchanges Gung Fu ideas with a fellow student at the Oakland Jun Fan Gung Fu School run by James Lee. George previously trained in Gung Fu for years in China as well as dabble in the martial arts here in the States before he met Bruce Lee.

George Lee with close friend and Sifu James Lee posing for the camera. Bruce Lee dictated the techniques that were supposed to line a follow up book to the earlier "The Art of Gung Fu". Due to numerous reasons; Bruce Lee's schedule did not permit him to complete the book.

George Lee going strong at 91

George Lee today at the young age of 91 practicing Gung Fu in his backyard in Castro Valley, California. George stays fit daily with either martial arts training, dancing or playing tennis. George Lee preaches the words that Bruce Lee once said, "Running water never grows stale". As you get older you must move, or if not, the body will break down. Running water never breaks down.

Certificate to George

To George Lee
In appreciation for your dedication, timeless effort and unselfishness to help your dear friend, Bruce Lee, achieve his goal to preserve and perpetuate his art. The Bruce Lee Educational Foundation thanks you for your lifelong devotion and dedicated service.

This scroll was presented to George in April 1999.

BRUCE LEE'S
TAO
OF
GUNG FU

拳

道

PERSONAL RECORD OF

George Lee

BRUCE LEE'S
TAO OF
CHINESE GUNG FU

振藩拳道

以無法爲有法

以無限爲有限

學生李湯新係加省 Richmond 縣人在館修練期滿準予升入第 二 級 此證

李振藩

一九六六年十一月廿七日

Date Nov. 27, 1966

This is to certify that

George Lee

is personally taught by Bruce Lee, and having fulfilled the necessary requirements, is hereby promoted to *second* rank in Bruce Lee's Tao of Chinese Gung Fu.

BRUCE LEE

Captured Moments

Oakland Gung Fu Class

(top) Bruce Lee center and George Lee picture left, posing with the Oakland Jun Fan Gung Fu School run by James Lee in first row third from left.

(bottom) Here we see James Lee's Oakland class posing for a picture after their hard workout. Notice Bruce Lee's friend and student Robert Baker far left who later went on to start in Bruce's film "Fist of Fury." James Lee second from far right.

Bruce in Oakland

Bruce Lee watering James Lee's lawn in his backyard in Oakland California. Bruce, Linda and Brandon lived with James for a while and become very close, almost like family.

Bruce Lee posing for the camera in Oakland California in Gung Fu pose. This picture is from a series of images that were to be used in Bruce's second book on Gung Fu. It never materialized, but there are talks that might make this book a reality all these years later.

Bruce in Oakland with James and Allen

(top) Bruce Lee visiting his friend Allen Joe at Allen's store back in 1966. Bruce enjoyed going there and Allen even showed him how to carve meat as a butcher.

(bottom) Bruce Lee with close friend James Lee Christmas Eve in Oakland at James house. They were very close.

Jim Lee's Birthday Party

(top) Bruce Lee along side his friend James Lee helping him celebrate his birthday party in Oakland California.

(left) James Lee cutting his birthday cake as Bruce looks on. A funny story about why we were all in suits and Bruce was wearing this t-shirt. One of the kids ate too much and got sick. Unfortunately Bruce was on the receiving end of this boy's sickness. We had an extra shirt in the car. Needless to say, Bruce was more mad about this shirt being a fashion sense guy than the boy who got ill.

(right) Bruce Lee, friends and family of James Lee look on as Jimmy is about to cut his birthday cake and share with all.

Bruce's Birthday Party

Bruce Lee hanging loose with his good friend James Lee in Oakland for Bruce's birthday party.

The four Musketeers from left to right, George Lee, Allen Joe, Bruce Lee and James Lee at Bruce's birthday party in a local Oakland Restaurant.

Bruce and James celebrating with Brandon at their side.

Linda's Birthday Party

Linda Lee celebrating her birthday in Oakland at a local Chinese restaurant with her son Brandon at her side.

Bruce and son Brandon watch on as wife and mommy Linda blows out the candles on her birthday cake as friends look on.

Dim Sum in Oakland

Bruce Lee and George Lee take time out for a picture after having Dim Sum with friends in Oakland, 1967.

Bruce posing for a picture while having Dim Sum with George Lee and others in Oakland.

From left to right, Bruce, Linda, Brandon and Bruce's sister Agnes Lee, enjoying Dim Sum in Oakland amongst friends.

At lunch in Oakland with Bruce Lee, Danny Inosanto and Allen Joe as George Lee takes their picture during Dim Sum.

James Lee

James Lee in Kung Fu pose. Jimmy Lee was a very special person to Bruce Lee on many levels, but most importantly, Bruce looked up to Jimmy as sort of a big brother at times. They were very close.

James Lee was in incredible shape as you can see here in this photo. He prided himself as a bodybuilder. Actually he and Allen Joe were great bodybuilders back then.

James Lee in stoic traditional wing chun pose. Bruce and Jimmy were very close friends. Bruce liked the fact that Jimmy had that toughness in him, a real street fighter. Bruce liked that.

Visit to Los Angeles

Bruce Lee and visiting friend from Oakland Allen Joe, standing outside the Los Angeles Chinatown Gung Fu School on College Street in 1967.

Bruce Lee standing with close friend George Lee outside the Los Angeles Chinatown Gung Fu School, 1967.

The Green Hornet Days

Bruce in bodybuilder pose in this promotional picture, 1966.

Bruce in pose on a Southern California beach where he was taking pictures to promote his fighting method.

Bruce Lee taking a rest from a long day of shooting images to support his fighting method. Son Brandon shows daddy how it's done. Bruce was a very loving father and felt family came first.

The Green Hornet Days

George, James and Allen, enjoying their vacation on the set of "The Green Hornet" with Bruce Lee.

Bruce Lee posing with George Lee's sons on the 20th Century fox Lot in front of the Peyton Place set.

Bruce Lee behind the scenes of "The Green Hornet" posing with friend James Lee with his son and daughter.

Bruce Lee and George Lee on the set of "The Green Hornet", 1967, posing for the cameras.

The Green Hornet Days

Bruce posing for the camera in 1966 at his Barrington Plaza apartment with Linda and son Brandon. This was done for promotional reasons for "The Green Hornet".

A) George Lee center, Van Williams left, Bruce Lee right outside the 20th Century Fox Studios posing for the camera after a long day shooting "The Green Hornet". B) From the cameras view, Bruce Lee throwing kicks with Van Williams on the set of "The Green Hornet" on January 1967. C) Bruce Lee and Van Williams taking a coffee break at the 20th Century Fox studios before filming "The Green Hornet". D) George Lee, Bruce Lee Allen Joe and James Lee visiting Bruce on the set of "The Green Hornet". E) Promotional picture with Bruce Lee, Adman West center and Danny Inosanto at Adam West's house.

The Green Hornet Days

A rare picture with Bruce Lee and Van Williams taking a break from filming "The Green Hornet" doing wing chun.

Bruce standing with friend Allen Joe behind the scenes on the set of "The Green Hornet".

Bruce taking a pose for the camera with tourist friends in front of the Peyton Place set at 20th Century fox studios where Bruce was close by filming "The Green Hornet", 1967.

Fighting Methods

Bruce Lee with Daniel Inosanto posing Jeet Kune Do style for the camera working on concepts for the Fighting Method book project.

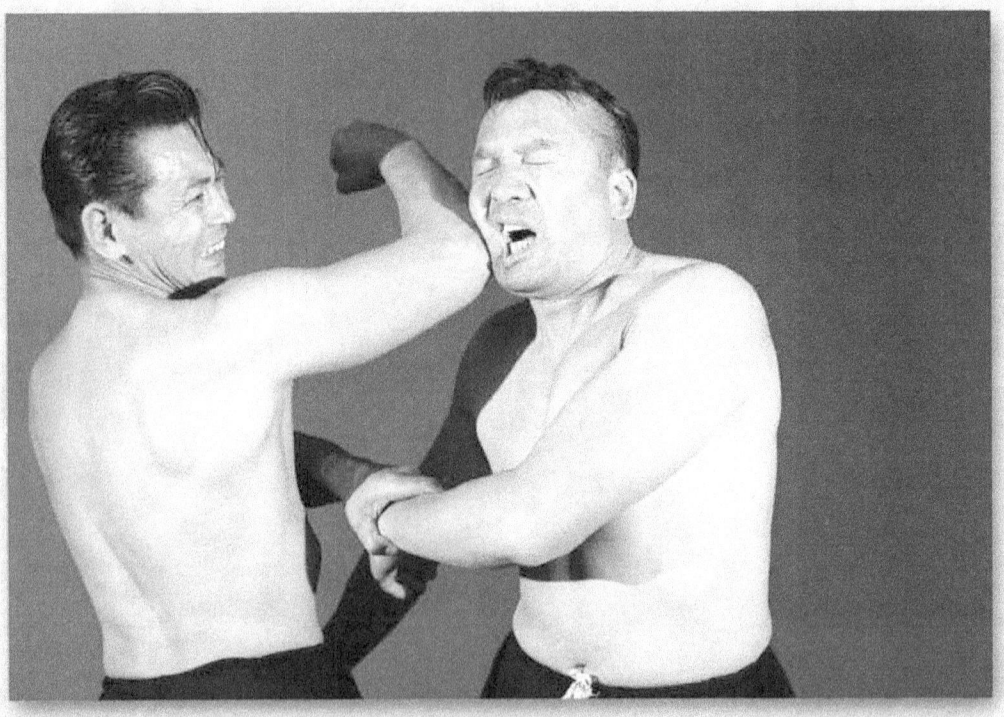

Allen Joe striking George Lee in this Fighting Method book picture. These times we shared all together as friends and confidants are memories to remember. They were great times.

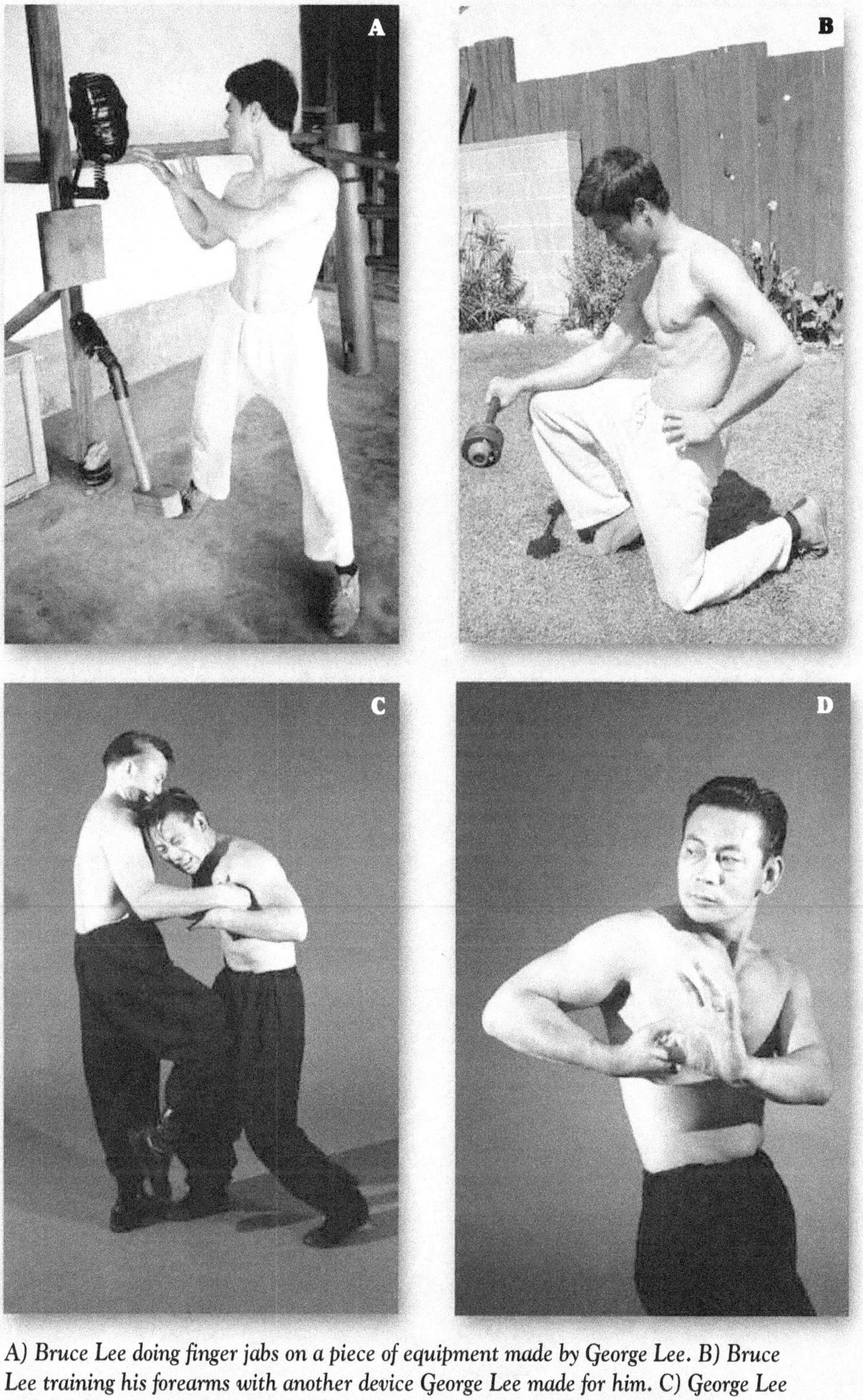

A) Bruce Lee doing finger jabs on a piece of equipment made by George Lee. B) Bruce Lee training his forearms with another device George Lee made for him. C) George Lee and Allen Joe in Jeet Kune Do battle. This image was to be used for Bruce Lee's Fighting Method books. D) Allen Joe in pose for the camera. Allen was a well-known bodybuilder back in the day and only one of the few Asian ones at that. He was always in great shape.

Bruce in Hong Kong

Bruce Lee in Hong Kong opposite a local Choy Lay Fut practitioner taken photos that were supposed to be used in a book Bruce had in mind. Bruce was to show the differences between the two styles.

Bruce Lee in 1963 upon his return home to visit his family, posing in Gung Fu form as his brother Robert takes the picture.

Bruce & Jhoon Rhee

Bruce Lee at the Jhoon Rhee Championships giving out a trophy to one of the event winners. Jhoon Rhee used to ask Bruce to help promote his tournaments to get people to come, Bruce always obliged him, and also knowing it helped him also promote himself.

Bruce & Robert Lee

Bruce Lee doing a flying jump kick over his brother, Robert Lee's head. This picture was taken by Linda Weintraub back in 1969. Bruce loved her skill as a photographer and trusted her to take intimate family photos as martial arts related photos as well.

Drawing by Bruce

One of Bruce Lee's classical drawings. Bruce made this drawing showing himself at an old age as a monk with philosophical presence. Bruce was a great artist.

When Bruce returned home to Hong Kong in the summer of 1963 to visit his family, he also investigated many of the various martial arts styles throughout the region and exchanged with some of the most well known martial arts instructors. The reason for this was, Bruce Lee was planning a follow up book to his now famous "Art of Gung Fu" book. Unfortunately, this book never came to light. This picture gives us a rare glimpse into what some of the content would consist of.

Special Dedication

I would like to make a special dedication to my dear brother Jake Lee. Jake was an incredible artist and in my opinion was one of the great American artists that now will be remembered for generations to come thanks to a special exhibit The Chinese American Museum put on. Not only were Jakes painting influenced by the Chinese culture, he also made his share of incredible American themed art as well.

I was fortunate to have been friends with Bruce Lee and I was honored that he trusted in me with the art I created for him to better his physicality. But to fully understand who I am as a human being, it is important to say that my brother was an important part of who I am then and now. As the years past, we saw and spoke to one another time to time, but there was always the unsaid words both of us knew, that we were family and cared deeply for one another.

So here is to my brother Jake Lee who was a true artist of life. I will always remember you and the legacy you left the world.

Love,
George

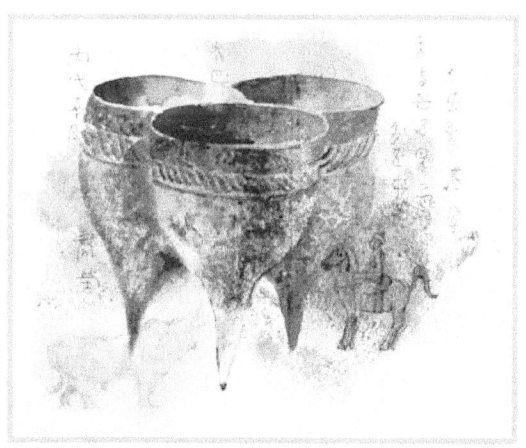

In Closing

In closing, I would like to say that I was truly fortunate to have met Bruce Lee. I hope when reading this book you've learned more about the "Little Dragon." These letters show Bruce Lee the man and Bruce Lee the legend, but most of all it shows Bruce Lee my friend. Bruce had other close friends and I'm sure they also have their own letters to share. I wanted to share my letters because I feel that the image of Bruce Lee can be one sided at times. It is important to recognize that Bruce Lee was a man that did great things and we must not forget he worked very hard to accomplish those great things. If Bruce Lee taught us anything at all it would be that hard work and relentless dedication will open up many doors with endless possibilities. Bruce had goals and he focused on those goals with the end result of accomplishing them goals. Bruce was not super human, he was just a super human being. Today there are many people throughout the world who have been touched by Bruce Lee in many different ways. As a good friend of his, I can assure you that Bruce would be proud to know that he has influenced so many individuals on the path to health and self exploration. There are great people like Dan Inosanto and Taky Kimura who were appointed instructors by Bruce, along with countless others like Ted Wong etc., who Bruce Lee instructed. I would like to say to these people that each of us has a piece of Bruce Lee in our memories and in our hearts. Over the years there have been disagreements on many levels regarding Bruce and how Bruce left his legacy. Let me just say that if we all take a step back and remember one moment that we shared with Bruce, and it makes us smile, then we all know we were part of his legacy. Let us remember that there are always two sides to a coin and that sometimes we do not have all the answers. I am just happy I can share moments in time with the many friends and fans of the late and great Bruce Lee.

George Lee

For further authentic information on Bruce Lee or the art
and philosophy of Jun Fan Jeet Kune Do®, please contact:

BRUCE LEE FOUNDATION
11693 San Vicente Blvd., Suite #918
Los Angeles, CA 90049

www.bruceleefoundation.org

The Bruce Lee Foundation, a California 501(c)(3) public benefit corporation, seeks to preserve, perpetuate, and disseminate Bruce Lee's life example, philosophies, and art of Jun Fan Jeet Kune Do ® through inspirational events, educational programs, martial arts instruction, and the Bruce Lee Museum. We believe that the Bruce Lee Foundation can enrich lives, open minds and break down barriers through the active proliferation of Bruce Lee's legacy of undaunted optimism in the face of adversity, unwavering humanism, mental and physical perseverance, and inspirational presence of mind toward the betterment of our global community.

www.ingramcontent.com/pod-product-compliance
Lightning Source LLC
Chambersburg PA
CBHW081355230426
43667CB00017B/2841